LET'S REALLY TALK ABOUT IT!

Adoptive and Foster Parents

LYVON M. CAMPBELL

CONTENTS

Introduction

The Let's Really Talk book line is a line of books designed to deliver honest responses to life experiences and hiccups. This book is not "one size fits all" for adoptive or foster parents. It is intended to provide tips or help, based on my personal experience as a parent. These words are not to negate or exaggerate any situations you may have experienced. The goal of this booklet is to provide points of similarity, that all parents may encounter during their journey to love their children, whether it is long or short term. All references whether they are clinical, spiritual, or life lessons seek to empower, inspire, and support the reader.

SPECIAL NOTE

The letter enclosed is written by Raven T. Love to be read by both parent and child when they can comprehend the subject matter enclosed. As an adoptee and advocate, Raven hopes to inspire each child to believe in themselves and begin the process to heal. The words written are from her heart and the objective was to say the words she needed to hear during her adopted childhood. Please read and process each word with the love, concern, instruction, care and inspiration that the author intends it to be.

I Am Not an Angel

When people find out I adopted kids from foster care and finalized a couple of private adoptions, their response is that I am "an angel and I saved my kids." I never agree with this mindset and often cringe when these words are spoken. Why do people think this, and more importantly, why do they feel it is ok to make such a disparaging remark in front of children?

The truth is my children saved me! I needed to love someone selflessly and without limits. I needed to affect the life of someone in a positive way. I needed to share my big, exhausting, supportive, over-bearing, and loving family with children. And I needed to be accountable to someone other than myself.

My children are the angels in my life. They have experienced loss, tragedy, and abuse but still find a way to love me every day. In most cases, their desire is to love and be loved unconditionally with permanence. I now redirect the narrative from me being a savior to letting people know how my kids save me every day.

Activity

Today take a moment and tell your children how they save you.

The Choice

"The decision to adopt for me had nothing to do with infertility …it was based on numbers."

I looked at the number of children in the foster care system versus the number of adoptions that were taking place. I looked at the outrageous number of sibling groups being split up to be placed in homes. I read, through tears, how many older children age-out of each state's foster system along with how many eventually become homeless.

My heart chose adoption because I could not see older children choosing to stay in the foster care system so their younger siblings could obtain a family placement. My heart wanted to see one sibling group stay together. My heart made the decision which goes against popular opinion and reason.

My choice to foster-to-adopt is unique and every parent has a different logic for taking this life journey with a child. Whatever the reason and no matter the obstacles, the decision to love a child and bring them into your family as your own is to be celebrated.

Thank you for choosing to foster! Thank you for adopting a child! Thank you for opening your heart! Thank you for sharing your family! Thank you for providing a forever home!

Activity

Take a few moments to share the reasons of your "choice" to unconditionally love your children forever.

Tough Transitions

For foster parents, each placement involves shifting the current children to welcome a new and often temporary family member. For the child, an adjustment to a new environment, neighborhood, parenting style, school, and list of friends can be daunting. How you manage their assimilation into their new surroundings determines their success all around. It is a vicious circle and never-ending juggling act as kids come and go, but how you push through and persevere can change the course of a child's future.

Adoption in my experience requires a wide range of adjustment as not only does the parent adjust, but so does the extended family. Ensuring your child is treated as an equal cousin, grandchild, and niece/nephew along with introducing them to friends, requires delicate handling with clear expectations and consistent communication. Determining how and when your child will be exposed to your life circle requires careful planning along with cautious movements. This life commitment is forever so everyone who touches your child's life must agree to your specified wishes.

Activity

Think of ways you have mastered or need to work on transitions. What tools have you learned along your journey?

Loving and Letting Go

Love is eternal and lifelong; however, for the foster family, it can be temporary. No one knows if a placement will be days, weeks, or longer so impacting a child's heart is critical!

How do you reach out in love to a stranger who may be scared, angry, confused, or reluctant to make a heart connection? Consistency and reinforcement are key components of relentless love. Also, being honest and extending the invitation to share feelings along with giving constructive feedback starts the process of trust, which leads to love.

It is vital and important to remember that love has failed them, hurt them, disappointed them, abandoned them, and confused them. Most of the time they do not love themselves or have a clear example of healthy love. One way to assess where your child stands on love is by asking or doing exercises on love and watching their response to plan your next move.

Activity

Think of ways that have worked for you when trying to connect in love to a child. Now share it with another foster or adoptive parent!

You are Their Parent

Friends and family may have a temporary view which manifests as a dissociation of you as the parent. This insidious attitude intuits that your child is "someone else's child that you took in." This mindset is further confounded when the birth family refuses to accept you as the forever parent and refers to you as the *foster family* after adoption. Many will profess that you should not make decisions as you are not the "real" parent. Lastly, there is the angry child who enjoys reminding you that you are not the real mom or dad during an angry diatribe or personal attack in writing.

No matter how it persists, the very idea that someone can consider you less than or different than a loving parent is hurtful and harmful. Although we cannot always change the thinking of those around us, we can protect our hearts by resting in the fact that we are indeed the God given parent.

If you are providing for, protecting, nurturing, correcting, feeding, clothing, and loving a child in your home, then you are the parent. No matter the length of their stay, no one can take this away from you or reassign your importance. Choose to understand that most speak from a lack of education and make the commitment to enlighten them.

Thinking and Planning

Who in your close or extended circle could benefit from viewing your role as a parent from a different perspective? What information or knowledge can you provide to help them adapt to a new way of thinking?

The Challenge to Connect

"Connecting with your child is vital in establishing trust and openness, resulting in an easier adjustment within the home and family. Figuring out which connection method will help you gain access to your child's mind and heart sometimes requires trial-and-error."

For some children, having regular conversations allowing them the space to share their feelings starts the process of breaking down the barriers. For other children, starting a writing journal may be the best way they can express their inner thoughts and feelings. In some cases, professional intervention is needed to foster the creation of a deep emotional connection.

It is important to always remember that your child needs to connect but may not have the tools or words to do so. As the parent, you are the bridge that will help them connect to their new life and family. It is helpful to learn all you can about their history, experiences, and health; then use that as the foundation to establish a connection.

No matter what they say or how they resist, your child wants to connect and become a part of a family. They will need time to process their past and deal with the resulting feelings. Then they must accept their current life cycle to start thinking and believing in their future. The amazing gift of this process is that you get to be the conduit that sets the standard for how they will adjust and securely establish a level of comfort, making it easy for them to respond to connection.

Reflection

Which tools do you use most to connect? Practical (life skills) or Professional (taught)? Which works better and why?

They Just Do Not Understand

"Everybody has an opinion. Some will share them formally while others may voice them in conversation. Some will think your choice to foster or adopt is amazing while others will think it is a mistake. The more opposition your decision generates, the louder the negative comments."

Throughout your adopting or fostering journey, you must make tough decisions regarding your child; that often includes maintaining birth family connections and visitation. In stressful situations your decisions may inadvertently affect your child. In my experience, I decided not to make certain people privy to my decisions, as it would cloud their judgement against my children. Unfortunately, my decision resulted in questions and judgements from those who did not have all the details.

The reality is most of the time privacy is the best option and everything does not need to be explained. Also, when your child is struggling, the last thing they need is a parade of their failures broadcast by everyone they encounter.

My best privacy practice involves sharing information on a need to know basis, along with structuring my visitations and outings so that issues can be addressed at home with confidentiality. I immediately communicated to my friends and family my decision to limit access in some areas and miraculously most understood. When people truly desire the best for you and your family, they can put aside what they think. That leaves room for them to hope and pray for the best outcome.

Reflection

Who in your life was initially opposed to your choice? Has that changed over time? If so, how?

Training and Education

Perspective parent training helps identify what choice they want to make, whether it be fostering or adoption. Learning the ins and outs of each option along with the requirements and time commitments helps inform the decision. **Fostering is not for every family, as it can involve emergency placements and quick removals, which can be hard on those who attach easily.** Visits coordinated with family and social workers on various occasions, require flexibility and understanding.

When considering adoption, the choices are plenteous as there are newborn, foster to adopt, international, private, and kinship options. The newborn process involves an agency and high costs as the birthmother's medical expenses are often part of the agreement. Foster to adopt tends to be cost effective as some states will cover most, if not all, of the adoption, lawyer, and home study costs. With this option a newborn is not guaranteed, and it may take years for parental rights termination and finalization. However, there are continuing education opportunities and special activities for foster children, plus higher education scholarships and tuition assistance in some states. International situations require authorization from multiple countries and the selected child may be chosen from a list of eligible adoptees. Private adoptions may involve the risk of scammers yet is also a direct way to connect with a birth mother. The last is kinship adoption, involving adopting a family member or the family member of a child you have already adopted.

While these are brief views of each option, during the education process, you receive information to help decide which choice to love is right for your family. The class and discovery time also may include activities and exercises to help the parent understand what the child feels along with resources to help during difficult times.

Activity

How did the training you receive help your parental journey?

The Importance of Assembling

Throughout my journey as an adoptive parent, I am fortunate to have the love and support of my family and friends. The advice given based on their experience as parents is helpful and constructive for the most part. Although it most always comes from a place of love, it sometimes does not apply to my family dynamic. Then I learned of adoption conferences and support groups which changed my world.

When I am speaking with parents who have similar experiences, I gain insight into my everyday life. Sharing our joys and pains and best strategies provides me with the needed parenting fuel to keep moving forward! I feel these parents understand me on a deeper level and I value these connections. In these settings I gain further education, practical knowledge, inspiration, and insight on parenting. Through the books purchased and classes taken, I have gained the needed tools to mitigate intense situations and feelings.

Attending a conference or class is like getting a breath of fresh air. A new perspective or outlook is what I need during turbulent times to renew my resolve and maintain my sanity. It is important to choose environments that will inform you and expand your knowledge base, while providing a safe environment to share your truth.

There are multiple ways to find free classes along with lists of resources offered by several agencies, including each state Department of Family Services. Conferences may have an attached attendance cost along with lodging and travel fees. While helpful, conferences are on an annual basis so finding local resources may be the best option for enhancement and support.

Question

How do you benefit from connecting with other adoptive and foster families?

Get Counseling!!!

"Counseling is imperative and necessary for adoptive and foster families. Unless you are a clinical professional, dealing with loss, grief, separation, anxiety, anger, and attachment require more skill than the average person possesses."

Each child comes as a gift wrapped in multiple layers of paper (experiences). As you unwrap each layer trying to access their heart, you must deal with each issue that affects their behavior and attitude. Not knowing what questions to ask may leave the parent clueless and worried. But a counselor can ask the correct discovery questions and develop a plan of action to reinforce positive outcomes.

As a parent I have tried to work out my children's issues with love and listening; however, in most cases I realized what they needed was far beyond my abilities. Through counseling, I learned better or effective ways to connect with my children. I also learned to parent each child based on their temperament, and that one-size does not fit all in treatment, reward, and punishment.

My counselor empowered my children to think and speak for themselves. They helped us connect to ourselves as individuals and together as a family. They helped identify problematic issues and behaviors. Then they helped me make informed treatment options for more serious issues.

There is no shame in admitting you do not have all the answers or know where to begin connecting with your new child. Do not be afraid to admit you need help even if you were parenting before this child. It does not mean you lack faith or hope, it means you want to exhaust all options in the best interest of your family.

Activity

List the ways counseling has helped you and your children.

Managing and Maintaining Birth Family Connections

"What are the rules on this? Do I have to? Must I? Will their involvement pose a threat to my family? Do I feel intimidated by them? Do I really want to do this? How do I do this?"

These questions are just a few that parents ask themselves when considering extending or opening birth family connections. The following are a few rules I developed over the years to help curb stress and proceed in peace with both families:

1. Set clear and concise boundaries, then communicate them to all parties involved.
2. Enforce boundaries.
3. Set a zero-tolerance policy for going against your wishes, with no exceptions!
4. Remember your only responsibility is to your child; so, their peace and protection is your only priority.
5. PROTECT YOUR CHLIDREN NO MATTER WHAT!
6. Monitor interactions with your child and pay close attention to their behavior immediately thereafter.
7. <u>Do not be afraid to limit exposure to threats.</u>
8. There is no rule that says you must maintain contact with anyone.
9. Do not let anyone force you into anything.
10. Do what works best for your family and revise as needed.
11. The only opinion that matters is the one that supports your family unit.
12. See rules #4 and #5

Hopefully, you can create an atmosphere where your child can experience both families and grow in a nurturing, mutually respectful environment. The goal for all sides must be to provide a garden of love for children to grow, while plucking out any weeds and defending against pests. Not everyone has this distinctive opportunity as each situation is unique, but if you do and it works…it is beautiful!

Background, History, DNA

"This subject carries a heavy weight, so let us establish that there is
no simple way to address it and no clear-cut method or
procedure for handling it."

Each child has a birth family which links them to people that often you as the parent have not and will never meet. This link carries their DNA and life history until they became your child; so how you handle it determines their long-term relationship with you. This connection contains how they behave, think, and love, no matter the age they come into your life. Their looks, body shape, and identity are established along with their lifelong health, which stems from their conception, pregnancy, birth, and subsequent nurturing.

For those who adopt without access to the birth family, the challenge comes with establishing access to information within acceptable guidelines. Whether through a case or social worker, requesting and receiving thorough background data may be limited especially if they had no contact with birth parents or family. In these situations, if the child is older, they may have some historical knowledge to share once they are open to releasing their past. If not, genetic testing is available for health diagnosis and future projections. For behavior and tendencies, watching and communication will reveal the needed answers daily.

When adopting from foster care, there is an opportunity to obtain information from past records, the case worker, and the family during visits or conversations. The collection of this information must be handled with sensitivity, based on understanding, and helping the child. It is important to follow the rules of confidentiality and discretion to avoid confusion and offense. Private adoptions often offer the most access to background knowledge as there is more access to, at least, the birth mother.

DNA and history cannot be downplayed, disregarded, or ignored and your children value that connection. They want to know there is someone in the world who looks like them and where they come from. This includes racial and cultural backgrounds as well. Create an environment of celebration for who they are so they will not feel that their existence is a problem (per my children).

Things I Wish People Would Stop Saying

This is the space to list all the things people say that are hurtful, that cause you anger, are judgmental, or are negative regarding adoption and foster care.

After you list each phrase or word, develop an informed and firm response for each one that changes the perspective of the person who said it.

Life Books and Memories

"Life books are wonderful ways for children to reflect over their young lives. A record of school and play pictures throughout their journey guarantees that they have no missing periods in their development and are simply precious!"

Once a child is either reunited or placed with a forever family, having a visual record of their life becomes important, especially when school assignments require baby or adolescent pictures. While life books can be a great source of history, it can also be a reminder of a life filled with broken connections and bad experiences. How one chooses to design and decorate these, books including the pictures chosen, evokes memories when each child views them in the future.

Some great ideas include creating a scrapbook collection with special days and times emphasized with bright colors and designs. Events like birthdays, holidays, and school events are days that can be decorated as their own page with matching embellishments. Another idea is to make special pictures of the day or time larger than others to draw the attention of the viewer.

An idea to include any pictures from their birth family helps to maintain the connection to any family they may be missing or longing to see. Also try involving the child in the creation of their book if possible. This gives them the opportunity to place special emphasis on any times that they feel is important to them. This is a time to learn what truly matters most to them which is a bonus when trying to establish connections with your child.

Life books may not be available for your child depending on the situation, when this is the case you are limited; however, there is a solution. If you know someone artistic let the child describe a person important to them and have a portrait created. You can have your child draw their own pictures from their memory then label and start creating their life book yourself. No matter the format, children will appreciate the effort and memories recorded as they age into adulthood.

Feelings of Giving Up

"It is normal to become overwhelmed and tired but when those feelings turn into feelings of giving up or disrupting, something must be done quickly."

Feelings that involve giving up are serious and often are the result of many weeks or months of trying to solve issues that are more than can be handled by the parent. No parent walks into an adoptive or foster placement with the intent of sending the child back. Knowing what your child has experienced or what they escaped from by being in your home is the fuel that pushes most parents to continuously find ways to handle the issues that arise.

Since there is such a negative and condescending view regarding placement disruptions, what would cause a parent to decide on this course of action? There is no easy answer for this question. It is important to note there are many types of disruptions that can occur, and some may not be the adoptive or foster parents' choice.

In domestic adoptions, the birth parent has a window of time following the birth to decide to parent. In other cases, the mental and emotional health of children suffering through issues of extreme violence, defiance, sexual misconduct, or psychological traumas may result in a break in the adoption process. It is hard for a parent to have to admit they cannot handle their child's struggles, after working with their agency, case worker, therapist, and employing other methods of helping their child overcome their traumas. This decision affects the child and your family, as both will struggle through the grief stages after separation.

There is an emotional and financial risk to each adoption, so finding an agency committed to reducing disruption on all sides and requiring counseling and case management should be the goal of every adoptive parent.

Tired? It Is Time for Respite and Rejuvenation!

Portions of this subject adapted from my book, Let's Really Talk About It! A 30-day devotional for Single Moms

Parenting takes a lot of planning, maneuvering, readjusting, and evaluating. It can take its toll on a parent resulting in physical and mental tiredness. Since most of parenting requires a large amount of mental exertion, it is not uncommon to feel physically weighed down. When you are feeling exhausted and drained its time to recharge.

Recovery via respite is a great way to recharge your body and mind. Respite provides the necessary siesta or rest for you to keep swinging in the parenting game. As it is a brief or short period of rest from something difficult or unpleasant, respite may be just what the doctor ordered for the tired parent.

Some ways to give yourself a time of rest may differ depending on your available options for childcare. A short drive alone enjoying scenery instead of running errands or having a meal alone away from the house, are some mini options. A longer rest may involve someone watching the kids overnight, a weekend, or a few hours, while you spend time reconnecting as a couple with quiet time alone. Recovery is the time taken to restore your mind, health, and body. Consider relaxing, meditating, sleeping, reading inspiring literature or just being still. Remember this is necessary and important to do on a regular basis.

Activity

Schedule a respite and recovery period for yourself.

A Job Well Done

"A parent's job is never ending. There may be no praise or even thanks for everything you do or the sacrifices you make. You do not parent for the praise and I know it is not required, but this is the space for you to receive a little acknowledgement."

If you love your children with all your heart…thank you! If you consider each child in your home part of your family, no matter how long they are there…thank you!

If you fight fearlessly everyday to nurture and protect your child…thank you!

For every visit you make possible…thank you!

For every time you dry their tears and try to replace them with smiles…thank you!

For creating a safe environment for your children…thank you!

For extending yourself beyond your limits…thank you!

****

Thank you for having the heart for children who need parents!
Thank you for creating forever families!
Thank you for working and discovering until you establish a connection with your child!
Thank you protecting them!
Thank you for creating healthy boundaries!
Thank you for keeping your word!
Thank you for opening your home and sharing your family!
Thank you never giving up!
Thank you for helping others become foster or adoptive parents!
Thank you for consistently learning and evolving to become better!
Thank you for being a parent!

The Forever Family

"All children need a forever home."

As an adoptive or foster parent your job is to create a safe, nurturing environment where they can grow. Within this home is where they will be loved and able to break down the walls preventing them from accepting the love that is awaiting them. In your home they will receive praise for their triumphs and correction for their mistakes. For many children, your home will be the place they learn to heal and be happy again.

They will acquire grandparents, aunts, uncles, cousins, and other extended family. Most importantly, they receive a forever family and home. This means for the rest of their lives they do not have to wonder where they belong. They have a place in your life and family and can come into the arms of safety anytime the world and life become too much for them to handle or even for holidays.

You are setting the path for their life! Your home will be the foundation of love and acceptance and you have the fortunate opportunity to change the course of how they will navigate the family they will create as adults.

Heartbreak

Heartache may come in the form of a child you have grown attached to suddenly being moved from your home without warning. You may hurt over the stories and experiences of the children you will parent, as you worry about their adjustment and future. As you try multiple strategies to break down the walls and work through their hurt, your heart leaps with each breakthrough and drops with each setback.

With adoption, specifically private ones, the opportunity of falling in love with an unborn child and having the birth mom choose to parent is a tremendous loss that can take a while to heal. Dealing with opinions and feelings against adoption from those closest to you creates conflict within the heart, as often pursuing this choice can strain relationships.

Rebuilding and picking up the pieces of a heart that is hurting and charting the course for healing is a daunting task especially when you are not fully aware of the hurt. Identifying the source then discussing and discovering the resulting feelings are key components in repairing the heart. Next building trust along with cautious handling of sensitive issues creates the foundation to establish a loving relationship between parent and child.

IMPORTANT

It is key to remember that often love has been tainted for children. Love for them has often looked like physical, emotional, or sometimes sexual abuse. Love has come in the form of abandonment and harsh treatment. Love has left them feeling as if they are not enough. Love has resulted in them being alone. Love has let them down. Love has broken their heart. Love does not work for their life. Love costs them too much and the longer they have been hurt, the less willing they will be to try loving again.

Processing Grief

Grief is the process of emotions in response to a loss. For the child it may be the loss of parental and familial bonds. For the foster parent it is the removal of a child, back to their parent or another temporary home. And, for the adoptive parent it is either the revocation of an adoption agreement or an extreme situation leading to a disruption or pre-adoptive termination.

There are stages to the grief cycle and the parent and child can go through different phases of each stage at the same time. Grief is experienced in our physical, behavioral, spiritual, social, and philosophical dimensions. Grief also evokes strong emotional responses; attendance to each area is necessary and mandatory for the healing process.

Grief can disguise itself as many feelings, such as agony, misery, sadness, pain, sorrow, anguish, trouble, annoyance, and distress. Since these feelings can masquerade as or mirror other issues such as depression, it is imperative to find the root cause of each feeling that weighs on the child or parent and address them individually.

The onset of grief is in response to a broken connection that often cannot be repaired or replaced. Most often the resulting feelings are intense and heartbreaking, due to the loss of a deep connection or relationship. The pain seems long lasting and often the person suffering feels that there is no end.

Question

How do you process grief? How you help your child identify and process their grief?

My Adoption Story—The Short Version

My first consideration of adoption came during my marriage in 2000. Both of us were experiencing fertility issues and our doctor recommended adoption as a way for us to become parents. We attended a community fair and met a representative from an agency, but I decided against the option at that time for personal reasons. After my divorce I came across the information again and started researching the statistics and outcomes for children awaiting forever homes. I decided to open my heart and family to the possibility of foster and adoptive parenting. I called then, partnered with Roots Adoption Agency, in Atlanta Georgia who specialized in finding homes for sibling groups and African American children, the largest number of children awaiting homes in Georgia.

Roots Adoption Agency, headed by Dr. Toni Oliver, gave me clear options and I chose adoption. I started my 12-week training, entitled Model Approach to Partnerships in Parenting, where I did exercises to put myself in the child's place and look at life through their eyes. Upon completion of the program, I was assigned a worker who completed my home study and final preparation to begin the search for my children. I never officially searched for any children as one day I received a call from one of my co-class facilitators asking me to meet two girls. I immediately said no as I wanted all boys! However, she convinced me to meet them and I arranged a meeting with their case worker.

I walked into the door a week later to meet my daughters and immediately knew they were my children. I left town later that day and learned of their emergency placement situation the following Tuesday. On Friday October 3, 2003, six days after meeting them, I received them into my home as a foster to adopt placement. I finalized their adoption two years later.

I did not know my daughters birth family and could not find them. I started going to a different church and after a few months I meet this nice lady I knew as Mrs. Sandra. A couple months later I found out she was my daughter's birth grandmother, which resulted in meeting their birth mother and entire family on Mother's Day 2007. We also discovered additional sisters, one living with other family and 18-month-old Fantasia. Almost immediately, she came to spend time with us and within six months started living with us full-time and the birth mother granted me custody of her.

During this time, I also worked at a company with over 3000 employees at my location. I met someone that worked in my department, on my team for a few months. A couple years later I received a call stating that person was pregnant and looking for someone to take the baby as she could not raise her. After speaking with her, sometime later I decided to take the baby that was due in a month. However, Imani had other plans as she came the day after I said yes in Texas. After an overnight trip and signed temporary guardianship papers, I returned home with Imani, April 12, 2008, at two days old.

During my training I said every week I wanted to adopt 5 boys and I became the mother of 4 girls. All I can say is love happened and I do not regret it. In August of 2015 we welcomed Xavier via birth, and he was just what we needed after losing my father and my kids beloved granddad. Everyone has a unique experience to share and I use mine to promote adoption. I experience trials, setbacks, disappointments, hurt, and frustration the same as any parent and I would still make the choice to parent all my children again. I am thankful for the support of my friends, my family, my mother, and the community that has worked with us over the years. The kids are 28, 22, 15, 12 and 5 now, so the joy of parenting continues!

-Lyvon

Thanks

I want to thank each of my five children for being patient and understanding as I grow into a better parent. Their love and support help me to move forward and having them cheer me on everyday is the best feeling. I truly do not know who I would be without them and I am grateful every day to be their mother.

I thank my parents and family for their love and support throughout my parental journey. Their immediate acceptance and non-partial treatment of my children created a circle of love that always makes them feel wanted.

I am thankful for my friends Theresa, Teresa, Nicole, Nikki and Katrina for the talks, advice, shoulders to cry on, and being great role-models for my children.

Lastly, thanks to my previous and current church families for helping me reinforce life lessons and Godly teachings.

I want to give a special thank you to Raven Love for opening her heart and sharing her story.

I am grateful for each of you and I love you.

www.ingramcontent.com/pod-product-compliance
Lightning Source LLC
Chambersburg PA
CBHW050819160726
48004CB00002B/920